($9.95)

CENTER STAGE

CYNDI LAUPER

By
**William Sanford
Carl Green**

Edited By
Dr. Howard Schroeder
Professor in Reading and Language Arts
Dept. of Elementary Education
Mankato State University

**Produced & Designed By
Baker Street Productions, Ltd.**

CRESTWOOD HOUSE

**Mankato, Minnesota
U.S.A.**

LIBRARY OF CONGRESS CATALOGING IN PUBLICATION DATA

Sanford, William R. (William Reynolds), 1927 -
Cyndi Lauper.

(Center stage)
SUMMARY: A biography of the popular rock singer and composer who was the first woman to ever put three singles from one album into the Top Three.
1. Lauper, Cyndi, 1953-   . 2. Rock musicians—United States—Biography—Juvenile Literature. [1. Lauper, Cyndi, 1953-   . 2. Musicians] I. Green, Carl R. II Schroeder, Howard. III .Title. IV. Series.
ML3930.L3S26   1986   784.5'4'00924 [B] [92]   86-11486
ISBN 0-89686-300-X

International Standard
Book Number:
0-89686-300-X

Library of Congress
Catalog Card Number:
86-11486

ILLUSTRATION CREDITS:

Cover: Ron Wolfson/LGI
Debra Trebitz/LGI: 4, 10, 28
Nick Elgar/LGI: 7, 27
Ron Wolfson/LGI: 13, 14, 24
Dave Hogan/LGI: 17
UPI/Bettmann Newsphotos: 18, 23
Patrick Harbron/LGI: 20
AP/Wide World Photos: 30-31

Copyright© 1986 by Crestwood House, Inc. All rights reserved. No part of this book may be reproduced in any form without written permission from the publisher, except for brief passages included in a review. Printed in the United States of America.

CRESTWOOD HOUSE
Hwy. 66 South, Box 3427
Mankato, MN 56002-3427
507-388-1616

TABLE OF CONTENTS

Introduction
    Four women all rolled into one rock superstar ..5
Chapter I
    Growing up in Queens, New York 7
    A singer, not a talker 8
    Music puts quarters in her pocket 9
    Always out of step 9
Chapter II
    The long climb up the musical ladder 11
    The rebel leaves home 11
    Singing with a disco band 12
    Fans like her style........................14
    The rocky road to the top 15
Chapter III
    An instant success 16
    An album goes "lead" 17
    A new boyfriend and manager 19
Chapter IV
    Riding high on the sound of the eighties 20
    Making a good song better.................21
    A near miss becomes a hit 22
    Branching out 24
Chapter V
    Cyndi just goes on being Cyndi..............26
    A passion for wrestling 28
    A life off stage, too 29
    The future is waiting......................32

Cyndi Lauper is a rock superstar.

INTRODUCTION

Four women all rolled into one rock superstar

Cyndi Lauper hit the rock music world like an earthquake. She jumped to the top of the charts in 1984, with a great album and an exciting video. Music fans couldn't stop talking about the red-haired singer from Queens, New York.

Cyndi has been around for a while now. How well do you think you know her? See if you can pick her out:

1. A rock singer runs out on stage, junk jewelry jangling. She belts out a song in a voice big enough to break windows. The audience loves her nonstop energy and good humor.

2. A camera crew is getting ready to film a rock video. A woman dressed like a high-fashion bag lady is telling the crew what to do. Then she jumps in front of the camera. In the next moment she's singing and dancing to a big rock beat.

3. It's a big night at the wrestling matches. In the ring, two women are fighting. But not all the

action is in the ring. The two managers, a woman and a man, are arguing with each other. The woman punches the man with a big foam-rubber fist. The crowd loves it.

4. Every year, *Ms.* magazine picks twelve "Women of the Year." The January, 1985, issue surprised a lot of people. One of the women chosen was a rock singer. In March, *Newsweek* put the same singer on its cover. Not to be outdone, *Time* called her one of the new female stars in rock music.

Okay, which one is Cyndi Lauper? Is she the hyper singer, the video producer, the wrestling promoter, or the woman of the year? If you're a Lauper fan, you already know the answer: Cyndi is all four women rolled into one.

In a field filled with talented people, Cyndi stands out. Like a fresh breeze in a stuffy concert hall, she's brought new life to rock music. Stardom didn't come easily for Cyndi, however. She had to fight her way to the top.

CHAPTER ONE

Growing up in Queens, New York

Cyndi Lauper (say it LAW-per) was almost born in the back seat of a taxicab. The date was June 20, 1953. The taxi beat the stork, though, and Cyndi was born in a New York hospital. Catrine Lauper named her baby Cynthia, but she soon was called Cyndi. The Laupers already had one girl named Elen. They later had a third child, a boy called Butch.

Cyndi recently posed for a picture with her mother, Catrine.

Cyndi lived in a section of New York called Williamsburg until she was five. People from many different countries made their homes there. There were Italians like Catrine, along with Germans, Irish, Jews, and Puerto Ricans. It was a tough place to grow up. Cyndi had to learn to take care of herself.

A singer, not a talker

Mr. Lauper worked as a clerk, but music was his true love. One of Cyndi's early memories is that of her father playing the xylophone for her. In fact, Cyndi began singing before she could talk. She knew the words to many popular songs by the time she was four. Today, Cyndi remembers that people weren't always thrilled by her singing. "She's not going to sing again, is she?" they complained.

In 1958, Cyndi's parents split up. Catrine moved her three children to the Ozone Park district of Queens. She worked thirteen-hour days as a waitress to support her family. When she came home, she was very tired. But she always tried to smile for her children.

Cyndi saw the sadness beneath her mother's smile. She also saw what was happening to the teenage girls on her block. Marriage and raising children turned them into tired old women. Cyndi vowed that she wouldn't fall into the same trap.

Music puts quarters in her pocket

Music was Cyndi's path out of Queens. She began by imitating pop singers, like Barbra Streisand and Eydie Gorme. But she didn't stop there. Cyndi also sang along with records of opera and blues singers. When she was alone and scared, she sang to "keep the ghosts away." She thought ghosts wouldn't kill a little girl with such a good voice.

Singing made Cyndi happy. But she also sang because it put quarters in her pocket. She went out on the street and sang for people passing by. Old women gave her money to sing songs from Broadway shows.

Cyndi never did fit in with the other kids. On her twelfth birthday she dyed her hair a rainbow of bright colors. Then she painted her eyelids pink and put on green lipstick. To complete her "look," she wore old clothes in a jumble of styles. Other kids laughed and called her names. Some even threw rocks!

Always out of step

Cyndi could take care of herself, but she wasn't happy. She says, "I was always out of . . . step with everybody else. I didn't know what was wrong with me or why I was so different. Nobody loved me. Nobody liked me." Even Catrine didn't know what to do for her daughter. She did go to church where she prayed that Cyndi would become "normal."

School wasn't any better. Cyndi flunked out of four schools in four years. Finally, Catrine scraped up some money and sent her to a Roman Catholic boarding school. Cyndi thought it was more like a prison. The nuns wanted her to be like the other girls. When she broke a rule, they pulled her hair, rapped her knuckles, or slapped her face. After six months of misery, she went back to public high school.

Through all of this, Cyndi never lost faith in her singing. She knew her voice would take her to the top. Somehow, she had to find a way to start up the ladder.

Cyndi has always been different!

CHAPTER TWO

The long climb up the musical ladder

As a teenager, Cyndi began writing her own songs. She also learned to play the guitar. At night and on weekends, Cyndi sang folk songs in the parks and at local clubs. People liked her singing, and she began feeling better about herself.

If her music was going well, nothing else was. School was still a problem. Cyndi went to the High School of Fashion Industries. The school put her into classes with other bright students who didn't get good grades. She tried to study art, but she didn't like the teachers. Finally, she dropped out of school.

The rebel leaves home

Home wasn't much better than school. Cyndi was a "street kid," and she had big fights with Catrine. She barely escaped serious injury in several auto crashes. Cyndi couldn't see any future in staying at home. She was only seventeen when she moved out. "I was packin' since I'd been fourteen, so it was about time," she says today.

The music world didn't put out the welcome mat. Cyndi had to work at odd jobs. At one time, she worked as a horse walker at a racetrack. Tiring of New York, she hitchhiked to Canada with her dog, Sparkle. She studied art and made drawings of the great outdoors. For weeks at a time, she and Sparkle camped out in the Canadian wilds.

Finally, the big city girl tired of the woods. On the way back to New York, she stopped off at an art college in Vermont. Cleaning dog kennels and working as a model helped pay the costs of going to college. Cyndi enjoyed her classes, but not the school. Any place with rules wasn't for Cyndi. It was the lowest point in her life.

Singing with a disco band

Back in New York, Cyndi tried music again. No one was waiting with a record contract. She had to find more odd jobs. This time, she worked as a secretary and sold karate lessons.

At last, Cyndi got a break. A disco band, called Doc West, hired her as a singer. The group played the music clubs out on Long Island. The audiences wanted to hear

Top Forty hits. Cyndi put her own music aside. She sang songs by people like Rod Stewart and Janis Joplin.

Music critics turned thumbs down on Cyndi. They said she was hyperactive. That much was true, for Cyndi was always in motion. She jumped up and down and ran all over the stage. Critics also said she looked like a little boy. There was some truth in that, too. Cyndi is only 5'3'' (160 cm) tall and she weighs only 103 pounds (46.7 kg). Despite the criticism, Cyndi refused to slow down. She put on platform shoes to make herself taller.

Cyndi has always been a hyperactive performer.

Fans like her style

Cyndi did win one battle. No one complained about the way she dressed. In the world of rock music, her

Fans love Cyndi's crazy clothes.

weird styles didn't look out of place. Most of her clothes came from a shop called Screamin' Mimi's. The store's customers liked her taste and became her first fans. They fell in love with her energy and her high spirits. Cyndi's pink eye shadow and flaming red-pink hair looked like a great new style.

The rocky road to the top

It was time for Cyndi to sing her own songs. She left Doc West and put together a rock and roll group called Flyer. The band soon had all the club dates it could handle. But the clubs were full of people who were heavy drinkers and made a lot of noise. Even with amplifiers, Cyndi had to scream to be heard. The screaming cracked her vocal cords.

It was 1977. Cyndi couldn't sing a note. Her career seemed to be over before it started.

Cyndi couldn't sing with cracked vocal cords. She left her job with Flyer and found a voice coach. Katie Agresta showed Cyndi how to use her voice. Slowly, her vocal cords healed. Cyndi couldn't read music, but she did the same voice exercises that opera singers use.

Katie helped Cyndi understand her own talent. She taught her how to make the most of a rock song. After a few months with Katie, Cyndi was healed both in voice and spirit.

CHAPTER THREE

An instant success

Cyndi was ready for her shot at the big time. Ted Rosenblatt, Cyndi's manager, booked her into a club in New York's Greenwich Village. She opened at Trude Heller's on St. Patrick's Day in 1977. The audience was full of rock fans who liked what they heard. Cyndi was an instant hit.

The "gig" at Trude Heller's opened another door for Cyndi. She met saxophonist John Turi there. In late 1979, the two put their own band together. Known as Blue Angel, the group played rockabilly (a mix of rock and western music). Cyndi and John wrote many of the band's songs themselves. Critics liked the band, but Blue Angel wasn't going anywhere. Without a hit record, the band would never become famous.

Cyndi and John made a demo tape and sent it to record companies. Steve Massarky, who managed the Allman Brothers, liked what he heard. He caught Cyndi's act, and thought her voice was magic. Blue Angel took Steve on as its new manager. Six months later, he signed the group to a contract with Polygram Records. Overjoyed, Cyndi and John began work on their first album.

An album goes "lead"

Polygram released *Blue Angel* in 1980. Cyndi and John wrote ten of the twelve songs on the album. For its part, Polygram spent a lot of money on publicity for the record. Rock stations played it, and the critics gave it good reports. It looked as though *Blue Angel* was about to take off. Meanwhile, the group picked up gigs as a warm-up act for the Ramones and for Joe Jackson. The band also made one of the first music videos. Their video, called *I Had a Love,* won a prize at a film festival.

Cyndi clowns with a puppet.

In 1985, Cyndi also won awards for music videos.

Cyndi and John rooted for their album to go gold or platinum. For an album, "going gold" means sales of 500,000 records. "Going platinum" means one million sales. Publicity and good reviews, however, couldn't save *Blue Angel*. In Cyndi's words, *Blue Angel* "went lead." The band's hopes sank with their record.

Polygram asked Cyndi to work as a single. She refused. As she said later, "Polygram wanted to . . . put cement go-go boots on me, so I couldn't do anything onstage." She made plans for a new Blue Angel album, but nothing worked out.

A few months later, Steve Massarky sued the band for $80,000 (US). The band broke up because no one had that much money. The break-up left Cyndi out of work and out of money. She took a job as a singing geisha-girl at a Japanese piano bar.

A new boyfriend and manager

Through all of this, Cyndi kept her head up. She knew Blue Angel's music was good, even if music fans weren't ready for it. Six months later, she met Dave Wolff. Cyndi remembers Dave as "funny and wacko." He soon became Cyndi's boyfriend and manager.

In 1983, Dave talked Portrait Records into signing Cyndi to a contract. The days when producers wanted Cyndi to copy other singers were over. Portrait agreed that no one should try to change her style. The company hired some talented musicians to back up Cyndi.

That left only the music itself. Portrait was gambling on an unknown singer. Could Cyndi measure up?

CHAPTER FOUR

Riding high on the sound of the eighties

The contract with Portrait gave Cyndi the chance to record her own album in her own way. She knew exactly

Cyndi finally got the chance to record an album her own way in 1983.

how she wanted it to sound. "I tried to reflect **this** time and **this** day," she said. "I wanted an electronic sound . . . I tried to cover all human emotions." To Cyndi, this was the sound of the Eighties.

The producers wanted some well-known names on the album. That's why Cyndi recorded songs by Prince and Tom Gray. But this was Cyndi's show. She worked with John Turi and Jules Shear on a wide range of music. *He's So Unusual* was a rewrite of a 1929 song, and *Witness* had a reggae flavor. The songs were well chosen. They let her sing everything from Fifties rock and roll to Eighties new wave.

Making a good song better

The song that made Cyndi famous was a Robert Hazard song called *Girls*. When Cyndi first heard it, she was angry. She thought the song "put women down," so she gave it "a different feel." She changed some words and reworked the melody line. The name changed, too. When Cyndi was done, *Girls Just Want to Have Fun* had become a theme song for modern women.

It takes more than songs to make a hit album. Portrait hired top people to do the art work and take the pictures. Cyndi made sure she had a vote in these decisions. She also helped name the album. To begin with, a friend telephoned the studio to ask about Cyndi. "She's wonderful!" the producer said. Cyndi heard him and laughed. "That's what we'll call the record—*She's Wonderful!*" she said. A studio engineer had a better idea. "No," he said, "*She's So Unusual.*"

A near miss becomes a hit

She's So Unusual came out in October, 1983. Portrait's press agents spread the word: Cyndi was going to be a big star. The music critics agreed. One review described Cyndi's "wild and wonderful skyrocket of a voice." Everyone loved the album—but it didn't take off. Was this album going to "go lead" like *Blue Angel*?

Luckily, Portrait had another trick ready. Two months earlier, the company had made a video for *Girls Just Want to Have Fun.* Cyndi had rounded up her family and friends and put them into the video. She even found a part for Sparkle. The cameras followed her as she sang and danced through the streets of New York. As Cyndi said later, "[The video] showed a girl having fun, yet dealing with her mother and father." The head of MTV looked at it and said, "This is a super video!"

MTV put the four-minute video on the air in December. That was the push Cyndi needed. The single of *Girls Just Want to Have Fun* quickly went gold (one

Cyndi received an MTV award for Girls Just Want to Have Fun.

million sales). It pulled the album along with it. The critics loved Cyndi's ability to make any type of song sound good. The hot-selling album led to a concert tour of Japan, Australia, Hawaii, and England.

Branching out

In February, 1984, Cyndi showed she was more than a singer. She put on a funny skit with Rodney Dangerfield during the Grammy Awards show. After that, she showed up on television talk shows. Johnny Carson and David Letterman had fun with her Brooklyn accent and

Cyndi puts on a funny skit with Rodney Dangerfield at the 1984 Grammy Awards.

off-the-wall humor. One writer said she had a speaking voice that sounded like a squeaky Minnie Mouse. That didn't bother Cyndi. If people didn't like her voice or her crazy outfits, that was their problem. *She's So Unusual* kept on selling. It went platinum six times over. By summer, *Time After Time* and *She Bop* had joined *Girls Just Want to Have Fun* at the top of the charts. No female singer had ever before put three singles from one album into the Top Three. Filmmaker Steven Spielberg liked Cyndi so much that he asked her to write and sing the title song for *The Goonies*.

Cyndi played to standing-room-only crowds when she went on tour. She was at her best in concert halls where she could be close to the audience. During her act, she danced all over the stage. Sometimes she climbed up on the loudspeakers. But it was her clear, true voice that won people's hearts.

The awards started piling up. In April, 1984, Cyndi won an American Video Award, as the Best New Female Singer. In September, she collected an MTV award for the Best Female Video. Those honors were just the start. In February, 1985, she picked up a Grammy as Best New Artist of 1984. She also won two American Music Awards and six American Video Awards. The little girl from Queens was now a rock superstar.

CHAPTER FIVE

Cyndi just goes on being Cyndi

Success hasn't changed Cyndi Lauper. "I'm not trying to be different," she says. "I'm just saying it's okay to be yourself."

For Cyndi, being herself means wearing what she wants to wear. She still goes "junking" at Screamin' Mimi's for clothes. Her outfits are just as many-colored and many-layered as ever. She also jokes about her jangling chains and belts. "People who dress like I do," she says, "need a chain cutter to get undressed."

Cyndi's age is one thing she doesn't joke about. Ask her how old she is. She answers, "What am I, a car?" The truth is that Cyndi turned thirty in 1983. She may be worrying that she's too old for her teenage fans. In the same breath, however, she tells herself not to take life too seriously. "If you get too serious," she says, "you could die of starch."

"If you get too serious," Cyndi says, "you could die of starch."

A passion for wrestling

Music isn't Cyndi's only interest. She also enjoys the excitement of pro wrestling. Her Grandpa Gallo turned her on to the sport when she was a little girl. Like Cyndi, wrestling is colorful and a little crazy.

One of Cyndi's best friends in wrestling is Captain Lou Albano. But even good friends fall out, or so it seemed. In July, 1984, Cyndi claimed that Captain Lou had been saying mean things about women. She said

One of Cyndi's good friends is wrestler Captain Lou Albano.

her wrestler (Wendi Richter) could beat Captain Lou's wrestler (the Fabulous Moolah). MTV put the match on television.

At ringside, Cyndi and Captain Lou traded more insults. Then Cyndi punched him with a big rubber fist. That set the stage for the wrestlers. Wendi won a close match as Cyndi cheered her on. Afterward, Cyndi and Captain Lou went to a party together. The whole show was a big put-on.

A life off stage, too

Cyndi always knew that her looks wouldn't open many doors. Instead, she relied on her singing and being different. Even as a child, she knew that her voice was a special gift. "My voice has always been stronger than my body," she says. Today, critics marvel at her four octave range and perfect pitch. As for being different, Cyndi doesn't copy anyone. Her fans love it when she shows up with pea-green lips and tiger-striped eyes.

Cyndi also likes being called a woman of the Eighties. She earned that honor fairly, too. The music business is mostly run by men. But Cyndi makes her own decisions. "If something was good enough for a man to do," she says, "then it was good enough for me to do." That doesn't mean that she doesn't like men. She and Dave Wolff are a good team, in public and in

Cyndi clowning with another wrestling friend, Hulk Hogan.

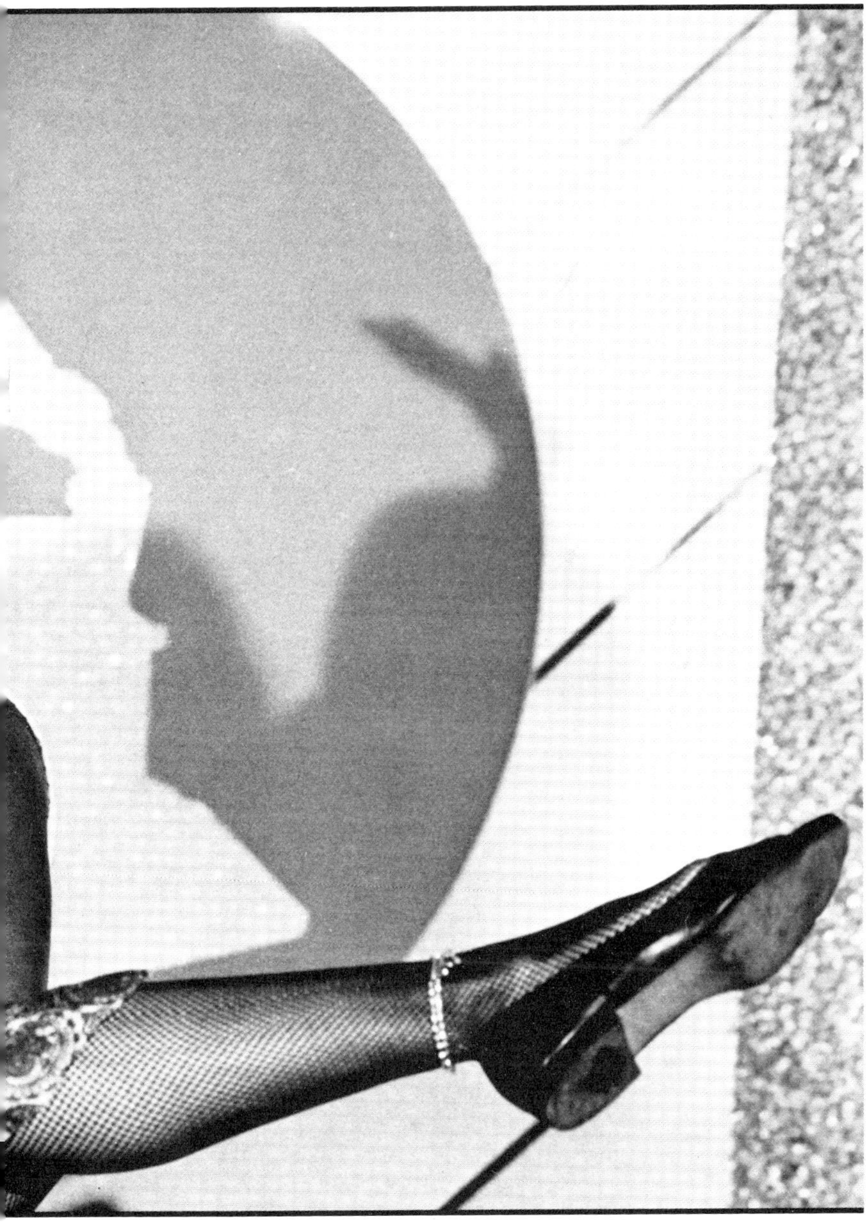

private. Cyndi's not against men; she's **for** women.

Her busy career doesn't leave Cyndi much free time. When she's not working, she likes to sleep. "Sometimes I'm so tired I don't feel anything," she complains. When she's not resting, she watches old movies and goes shopping. She doesn't have a car or a driver's license. That's "my gift to society," she says, pointing to all the accidents she's had.

The future is waiting

What does the future hold for Cyndi Lauper? Her second album has been delayed several times. Cyndi knows that her fans expect something even better than *She's So Unusual*. Topping an almost perfect album is never easy. She doesn't want to put out a bad record just to meet a deadline.

Cyndi's sure that she'll make more videos, or even a rock movie. They fit her style. "I love doing the videos," she says. "My work is full of emotion. It's real, you can touch it."

Like the girls in her songs, Cyndi's having fun. Her success is sweet because she won it on her own terms. "Nothing can beat that," she says.